♥ For Julie, my forever pen pal

♥ For Mallory, my favorite camper

© 2023 Creative, Simple Wonder Press
All rights reserved.
This book or any portion thereof may not be reproduced or used in any manner without the express written permission of the publisher.
ISBN: 978-1-7370386-7-2
kimberfoxmorgan.com

Chipper Sends Sunshine

Written by Kimber Fox Morgan
Illustrated by Kim Sponaugle

Chipper, Marta, Gus, and Scout will leave the arctic air

They planned a week at Bright Stars Camp - and boy, were they all glad!

They made new friends and had a blast
- best time they'd ever had!

Chipper paired with Sidney for the contests played each day.

Gus and Bruno bonded over splashing water play.

Scout and Peyton found their groove just soaking in the sun.

Ike invited Marta on a friendship-building run.

"Friends for life!" the campers said.
They vowed to always write.

They shed some tears at leaving time. Those hugs were super tight.

At home the friends were looking back at camp and feeling glee,

And planning how to keep their cool adventure running free.

Chipper shared ideas, plus the moments that he'll miss:
"I'll write a letter to my pal and seal it with a kiss"

But Chipper's letter was returned. He had the wrong address.

"If Sidney thinks I'm not his friend - oh, that would be a mess!"

Gus sent arctic snow to cool his water-loving friend,

but Bruno opened soggy notes, which nothing helped him mend.

Scout found treasures for her friend - some shells and special rocks.

The rocks fell through a hole, and Peyton had an empty box.

Marta didn't fare much better sending flowers from the trail.

Over time the flowers died, and Ike got stinky mail.

The buddies met together and came up with something sweet.
They hoped to make their pen pals smile by sending them a treat.

With a kiss they sealed their mail
to give the postal clerk.

Sidney opened up his box and shed a happy tear.
His friend had sent the best of gifts.
He giggled with a cheer.

Bruno shyly unfolded the top of Gus's post,
but soon he knew he had received
the thing he wanted most.

Peyton hoped that Scout's new note would make her laugh and smile.
It didn't disappoint her. She was grinning for a while.

The mail arrived at Ike's tall house,
and with a tug and lift,
he pulled the treat from Marta out.
It was the perfect gift.

Letters traveled back and forth with jokes across the miles, counting down the days until they'd share their laughs and smiles.

Camp had made them best of pals, a friendship of the heart.

Letters helped to close the gap they felt while far apart.

If you've found a friend to love, try not to let them go.
You can mail a friendly **hug** and help the friendship grow.

CPSIA information can be obtained
at www.ICGtesting.com
Printed in the USA
JSHW070830190423
40557JS00002B/22